THE REAL GOSPEL

Bert M. Farias

A Holy Fire Ministry Publication.
Printed in the United States of America.

ISBN-13: 978-0615649597
ISBN-10: 0615649599
Library of Congress data is available for this title.

CONTENTS

FOREWORD..7

INTRODUCTION: A DREAM..9

Chapter 1 - THE DEIFICATION OF MAN............................11

Chapter 2 - THE MODIFICATION OF THE GOSPEL............25

Chapter 3 - THE OFFENSE OF THE CROSS........................37

Chapter 4 - THE JUDICIAL ASPECT OF THE CROSS...........53

Chapter 5 - THE GOSPEL OF POWER...............................65

Chapter 6 - THE MESSAGE OF THE CROSS.......................75

Chapter 7 - A CHRISTMAS LETTER 79

ABOUT THE AUTHOR...83

FOREWORD

THE REAL GOSPEL, by Bert Farias, is a must read for everyone, from those seeking to know God, to those preaching Christ's Gospel. This is a true presentation of the Gospel, and not just a commentary on one facet or an emphasis on an aspect of the Gospel. It is a solid presentation of the essential truths that explain why we need a Savior, how Jesus saves us, and how to receive Him. Bert Farias brings back into focus, the truth about sin, its damning effects upon mankind, and why the cross of Calvary was necessary and sufficient to provide salvation for us. He then, clearly and courageously, lays out the plain truth of the Gospel and about what is missing in so much of the modern approach to presenting Jesus Christ. This book, in furnishing the full and true Gospel message, reveals why so many Christians and churches lack power, endurance, and character.

THE REAL GOSPEL is truly a book for this hour. The constant popular emphasis on making the Gospel relevant to our culture is obnoxious and misguided because it's based in the error that modern people must be reached on the humanist level of their self-interest – that they are otherwise incapable of patiently hearing the Gospel before becoming offended by its demands for righteousness and holiness. This book clearly defeats that error by showing that the real Gospel is "the power of God unto salvation," for all people, for all time.

From my experience, having served full-time in pastoral, missionary, and church-planting ministry since 1975, this is one of the best, well-balanced presentations of the Gospel of Jesus Christ that I have come across. I will be highly recommending it to my home congregation and missions churches.

Nick Champlin, Faith Christian Church, Clearwater, FL
Nigeria-Ijaw Mission, Niger Delta, W. Africa

INTRODUCTION: A DREAM

Recently the Lord reminded me of a dream I had a number of years ago. He quickened me to pray concerning the importance of the dream. In the dream I was walking with a pastor on church property where many were gathered in a picnic-like fellowship. As we were walking I noticed a small cookhouse where the pastor took me in. All kinds of food was being prepared, several dishes of which I was familiar with from my years on the mission field in Africa. As my eyes looked upward I saw shelf after shelf of warm cooked food that had been stored, but not served. I asked the pastor why he wasn't serving that food because the people needed it.

I was shocked when he replied, *"This is strange food to them."*

"But it's being wasted here," I said.

Then the pastor and I walked back out onto the church property as he continued to show me more of the facilities. When we crossed over a small garden bridge I saw weeds and tares sprouting up from under the bridge. As I looked around I was seeing these same weeds and tares growing up all over the property, so much so that our feet became entangled making it difficult to walk.

When I woke up from this dream I was distressed in my heart, and I inquired of the Lord as to the dream's meaning. He told me that the weeds and tares represented festering sin, complacency, and compromise resulting from a neglect of certain messages and truths that His body was not receiving.

"For I have not shunned to declare to you the whole counsel of God" (Acts 20:27).

9

"If you instruct the brethren in these things, you will be a good minister of Jesus Christ, nourished in the words of faith and of the good doctrine which you have carefully followed" (1 Tim 4:6).

"Preach the word! Be ready in season and out of season. Convince, rebuke, exhort, with all longsuffering and teaching. For the time will come when they will not endure sound doctrine, but according to their own desires, because they have itching ears, they will heap up for themselves teachers; and they will turn their ears away from the truth, and be turned aside to fables" (2 Tim 4:2-4).

These verses speak of "the whole counsel of God", "words of nourishment", and "sound doctrine" that are necessary for a holy, fruitful, Spirit-filled walk for every believer.

Carolyn Farias

Chapter 1

THE DEIFICATION OF MAN

"During times of deceit, telling the truth becomes a revolutionary act."
George Orwell

"Oh, that you would bear with me in a little folly—and indeed you do bear with me. For I am jealous for you with godly jealousy. For I have betrothed you to one husband, that I may present you as a chaste virgin to Christ. But I fear, lest somehow, as the serpent deceived Eve by his craftiness, so your minds may be corrupted from the simplicity that is in Christ. For if he who comes preaches another Jesus whom we have not preached, or if you receive a different spirit which you have not received, or a different gospel which you have not accepted—you may well put up with it!" (2 Cor 11:1-4)

At the beginning of the writing of this book I was simultaneously engaged in a friendly spiritual dialogue with a former childhood friend on Facebook. The conversation was spawned from a status I had just posted on my profile page the day before. What I shared was a diagram of two photos, exposing in a dichotomy, the hypocrisy of liberal values. The photo on the left portrayed two homosexuals in festive, colorful attire kissing each other in what looked like a gay pride parade. Below the photo was the word "encouraged". The photo on the right portrayed two little children sitting at their desk in school with hands folded in prayer. Below that photo was the word "unacceptable". In other words, Liberalism encouraged homosexuality while deeming school prayer unacceptable.

My friend pointed out that the photo of the children was upsetting to him as he believed that no one should discourage children from praying, but the one of the homosexuals kissing didn't bother him.

Here is the exchange between us:

Friend: "As for the picture on the left, get over it. Homosexuality has been around for hundreds of years, and it will remain for hundreds of years to come. In the grand scheme of things, it's not a big deal."

Me: "The loyalty of true devoted Christians is to the truth and testimony of the Word of God, David. The Scriptures, which you probably doubt are God-inspired, are clear on homosexuality. It is an abomination to God (Leviticus 18), unnatural (Rom 1), and in opposition to God's nature and sacred order (Rom 1). No one in this lifestyle can inherit the kingdom of God (1 Cor 6:9-11), but will incur God's wrath unless they repent and seek help and deliverance. Homosexuality has always been rejected throughout history. It is biologically abnormal and gay people know that deep inside. They are forever trying to get society to accept it in order to remove the heavy burden of guilt they are under. The good news is God loves them, did not make them this way, and can change them and set them free. I know a number of people who were in that lifestyle but are living normal lives today. David, I say this to you with all love and kindness: To say that homosexuality is no big deal reveals to me that you are not a true Christian and have not yet been enlightened and come to repentance from sin and faith toward Jesus Christ. I also discern that because you know a number of whom you say are "good" people in this lifestyle, you have concluded that it must be okay. But once more, this too is error. Our loyalty must be to the truth of the inspired Scriptures, and not to men, be it loved ones or close friends. Do not be deceived. He that is born of God cannot practice a lifestyle of sin because his nature has been changed by the grace and power of God (1 John 3:9)."

Friend: "The church I grew up in, and continue to attend on a very regular basis is an open and affirming church. During my faith journey in this church, I have been a deacon, an elder, and president of our church council. Since our church is open and affirming, and my Christianity has been brought into question, one can conclude that the faith of all 763 members of our church is in question based on your position. I choose to love and respect all people regardless of their own faith, culture, or lifestyle. I have been married to women twice, and divorced twice. If two men or two women are perfectly content with each other, and truly love each other, I am perfectly content in that and would be supportive of them in any way I can. I often think the manual used in justifying our individual faith or agenda can be extremely damaging. We will agree to disagree, and I have enjoyed this little debate. I will forever choose to love and respect all people regardless of the journey they choose to take while on this earth."

Me: "David, that is not my position, but the position of the Word of God and the Scriptures that I referenced. That is the manual! And not adhering to the manual is what is extremely damaging!!! Can anything be clearer than 1 Corinthians 6:9-11? Ephesians 5:5-6? Rev 21:7-8? And if time permitted I could list a host of many other scriptures. This is the great deception of Christianity in America today, and one that I am currently and passionately speaking on and writing about. I know of what I speak. I love and respect all people for they are God's own creation, but I don't respect people's sinful lifestyles that are contrary to the Word of God. True love and respect speaks the truth, and warns people of death, hell, and the judgment to come commanding them to repent. Be not deceived, David! Heaven and earth shall pass away, but God's eternal Word will last forever. Our faith must be based on that Word."

My friend's comments actually represent a large segment of professing Christians in America today, both on the liberal and even now on the conservative wing. His comments are also indicative of how secular humanism has penetrated in one form or another into the mainstream of our culture and infiltrated many of our churches; be it denominational, evangelical, and even Charismatic/Pentecostal churches. This wide departure from the faith, in what has now become a sort of post modern Christianity in America, signals the death knell for many. The celebrated philosophy of the day of "no absolutes, no right or wrong – whatever makes you happy – be tolerant and accepting of everything and everyone" is eroding the core of Judeo-Christian Biblically-based values, and greatly weakening real Christianity in America and in other nations as well. I fear for the multitudes of the deceived who shall soon be the deceased. This could indeed be the final acceleration of the great apostasy the Bible speaks of will happen in these last days.

"Now the Spirit expressly says that in latter times some will depart from the faith, giving heed to deceiving spirits and doctrines of demons" (1 Tim 4:1).

"For the time will come when they will not endure sound doctrine, but according to their own desires, because they have itching ears, they will heap up for themselves teachers; and they will turn their ears away from the truth, and be turned aside to fables" (2 Tim 4:2-4).

By the world's standards, my childhood and now Facebook friend, is a good church going citizen. I can tell you that he is nice and kind to people, willing to go out of his way to lend a helping hand to anyone who needs it, well-liked and even esteemed by others, but he is still deceived. His stand on homosexuality and sin is unbiblical, ungodly, and most of all eternally fatal. His beliefs are the product of a false gospel.

Think of it: Here is a man, now in his 50's, who's been in the same church all his life, has held various positions in the church, and still has not been converted and entered into the real faith. Like millions in America, he is a product of a liberal theology birthed from secular humanism that can't tell you for sure, or *won't* tell you for sure, if there's a heaven and a hell, but will try and keep you happy while you're still alive, all in the name of God and love. This is why a person can be a member of a church and yet be living a gay lifestyle. He can carry a Bible and be in an adulterous affair. He can adhere to a form of doctrine but have no peace.

The center of the real gospel is that Jesus came to save humanity from their sins, and that means much more than just forgiveness. Proof of salvation is regeneration. Proof of grace's power and reality is a transformed life. Proof that Jesus is your personal Lord and Savior is freedom from the bondage of sin.

"And she will bring forth a Son, and you shall call His name JESUS, for He will save His people from their sins" (Mat 1:21).

The name Jesus means "The Lord saves". He doesn't only save from hell, but he saves from sin. The problem is not hell. The chief problem with man is sin. Sin is what separates man from God. Sin is the reason for redemption. For this purpose Jesus came, was crucified, shed His blood, died, was buried, and rose again. Hell is simply God's eternal penalty or punishment for sin. When we only proclaim freedom from the penalty and punishment of sin without also proclaiming freedom from the power and dominion of sin we fall short of the complete gospel, and we leave sinners unchanged.

Any gospel that waters down the sin problem, fails to mention it, deal with it, confront it, and offer a full deliverance from it is a false gospel. Although God is very merciful and can still save some who only hear a partial gospel, the right proclamation of the gospel increases our chances manifold of getting maximum results. If we are going to improve on the statistic that only approximately 10-15% of sinners who respond to some kind of invitation to be saved actually remain faithful to God, we are going to have to preach the real and complete gospel.

One of the great failures of our contemporary gospel today is the failure to deal adequately and thoroughly with sin, and call both sinners and saints to submit to the Lordship of Jesus Christ unconditionally. Calling people to *confess* Jesus as Lord without equally calling them to *submit* to His rule is softening the gospel to give it an easy appeal. To say it yet another way, proclaiming only the *forgiveness* of sins and Jesus as Savior without proclaiming *deliverance* from the power of sin and Jesus as Lord, is to fall short of the true gospel of grace. The grace of God not only forgives a man, but also changes him and empowers him to live in obedience to the rule of God.

The epidemic of secular humanism has infiltrated much of the Church, and it is spreading like an infectious disease. The best humanism can do is keep man happy in his sins and help him to manage it. It tells him what he wants to hear rather than what he *needs* to hear. It affirms him with a false, mushy kind of love that will eventually damn his soul. I don't know about you, but I would rather hear a painful truth than a comforting lie that will damn my soul. Right is right no matter how many people oppose it, and wrong is wrong no matter how many people endorse it.

To better understand the philosophy behind humanism let's carefully analyze a portion of my friend's comments:

"I choose to love and respect all people regardless of their own faith, culture, or lifestyle. I have been married to women twice, and divorced twice. If two men or two women are perfectly content with each other, and truly love each other, I am perfectly content in that and would be supportive of them in any way I can."

There is a grain of truth in these comments. Much of America would accept these statements today. Although it is godly and noble to love and respect all people regardless of their faith, culture, and lifestyle, we should not love and respect any faith, culture, or lifestyle that is in direct contradiction to the Lordship of Jesus Christ and the standard of the holy Scriptures. How can we respect any faith, culture, or lifestyle that eternally separates people from God and takes them to hell to perish forever?

It seems that after two failed marriages and subsequent divorces that my friend has adopted the philosophy of just being happy. He also accepts and even supports the gay lifestyle, and the thought of same sex couples living together in marriage doesn't bother him, as long as they are content or happy. As a matter of fact, this pursuit of happiness is the root cause for the divorce rate now being as high among professing Christians as it is in the world (again, the result of humanism infiltrating the Church), and for gays promoting their agenda so aggressively, not only in society but in churches as well (there are now gay churches popping up everywhere who ordain gay clergy to the ministry).

In regards to divorce, rather than accepting it as even an option, hating it as God hates it, working things out in honor of God and the family, Christians allow it and condone it as long as it adds to their own personal happiness and convenience. The same thing is true of homosexuality. *This is humanism —an agenda without concern for what is right in God's sight —the enthronement and glorification of self.*

The dictionary definition of humanism is this: The denial of any power or moral value superior to that of humanity; the rejection of religion in favor of a belief in the advancement of humanity by its own efforts.

After reading that definition you might be thinking, "Hey, Christians don't deny a superior power (God) and moral value, or reject religion!" But remember that humanism is the prevalent thought in the Western culture largely shaped by the mainstream media, and not seen or discerned by the multitudes. Due to its Satanic origin and nature it is deceptive. Humanism is the philosophy of our day that has infiltrated Christianity. It is very subtle, akin to the proverbial frog in boiling water. If you drop a frog into hot water it will immediately jump out. If you put a frog in cool water and slowly heat it, it will stay and die because it does not discern the sudden heat.

The majority of people in the West have not denied God per se or rejected religion, at least not in word or form, but in deed and in actions they undoubtedly have. Just the one example of same-sex marriage proves that. What was unthinkable 50 years ago has now been legalized in a number of States. *It is not the outright rejection of God or religion that signals a radical change in the Western culture, but the change in the motivation of the hearts of the people.* The wealth of any nation is the hearts of the people.

Humanism defined as a motivation of the heart is this: The end of all existence is the happiness of man. In other words, all of creation exists for the happiness of man. God reigns in heaven for the happiness of man. Jesus Christ came from heaven for the happiness of man. The angels exist for the happiness of man.

Again, you may be asking: "Is there anything wrong with being happy?" and "Does God not want us happy?" Happiness is honorable and desirable only when it is a by-product of holiness and true submission to God, and not a primary aim or a means to an end. God does not exist to make man happy.

True Christianity is the glorification of God. The end of all things is the glory of God.

Humanism is simply the deification of man. In the Western world we don't worship idols of wood carvings and totem pole images, but we worship self; thus the reason our hard-drinking, drug-using, immoral celebrities are deified by the mainstream media and society. Even in their death, countless obituaries laud these celebrities' abilities and accomplishments while skipping over their extremely godless lifestyles. Most of these celebrities can't even sustain a brief marriage, can hardly remain briefly sober, but continue to rake in the extra bucks from their celebrity endorsements, which are carefully heeded by their adoring, senseless fans who worship them. Humans have a need to worship something so it might as well be a better me or a superior you.

Even though at our very core we were created with an innate desire to be God-centered human beings, as a society our rejection of God as worthy of our worship has opened the door to increasingly foolish brands of polytheism, eastern religions, mysticism, and self-help gurus, all stroking the already inflated egos of our population and informing them of the latest religion that's all about *you.* These religions and philosophies have penetrated our Western culture and are eroding the influence and impact of Christianity.

As a further example of the progressively inordinate worship of self in our Western culture, let's examine the magazine industry to illustrate this evolution, especially throughout the last century. Decades ago there was a birth of a magazine in America called "Life" that was very popular. Later a new magazine was published that superseded "Life" called "People". Well, since "Life" is all about "People", the new magazine title made perfect sense. Something then changed in our inner consciousness and the industry took advantage of it, which necessitated a third magazine publication called "Us". Finally, as the motivation of the heart of American culture continued to spiral downward, alas, today you can walk through airports and observe on magazine racks in stores the latest new magazine called "Self". Coincidence? I don't think so.

This illustrates the gradual, ever-so-subtle change in the motivation of the hearts of our Western culture and the evolvement of it into such a preoccupation and an exaltation of self – an even stronger brand of humanism called narcissism where people's bodies and nakedness are glorified. We worship celebrities, singers, sex symbols, pop star divas, and athletes, and these become our heroes and our gods regardless of their often-times questionable character and lifestyle. We save the whales, the eagles, the bears, the trees, and mother earth, but we kill babies. And yes, we encourage homosexuality and now same sex marriage, but outlaw school prayer. This is the rotten fruit of secular humanism, and it is killing Western civilization as generations past have known it, and as I've repeatedly stated, infiltrating, infecting, and greatly weakening the Church.

Humanism is the betrayal of the ages and is in direct contrast to the gospel of Jesus Christ and to Christianity. It's been around for thousands of years, before creation as a matter of fact. It was born from rebellion in the heart of Lucifer before the creation of man.

"How you are fallen from heaven, O Lucifer, son of the morning! How you are cut down to the ground, you who weakened the nations! For you have said in your heart: 'I will ascend into heaven, I will exalt my throne above the stars of God; I will also sit on the mount of the congregation on the farthest sides of the north; I will

ascend above the heights of the clouds, <u>I will</u> be like the Most High.' Yet you shall be brought down to Sheol to the lowest depths of the Pit. Those who see you will gaze at you, and consider you, saying: 'Is this the man who made the earth tremble, who shook kingdoms, who made the world as a wilderness and destroyed its cities, who did not open the house of his prisoners'" (Isa 14:12-17)?

Lucifer asserted his own will above God's will. He deified himself to be as God. Then after his fall from heaven he subtly disseminated his humanistic philosophy, the ascension and exaltation of self, into Eve's ears.

"The serpent was more cunning than any beast of the field which the LORD God had made. And he said to the woman, "<u>Has God indeed said</u>, 'you shall not eat of every tree of the garden'?" And the woman said to the serpent, "We may eat the fruit of the trees of the garden; but of the fruit of the tree which is in the midst of the garden, God has said, 'You shall not eat it, nor shall you touch it, lest you die.'" Then the serpent said to the woman, "<u>You will not surely die</u>. For God knows that in the day you eat of it your eyes will be opened <u>and you will be like God,</u> knowing good and evil" (Gen 3:1-5).

Notice how Lucifer, now Satan, deceived Eve. He made her doubt the Word of God by making these three core statements:

"Has God really said not to eat of every tree of the garden?"

"You will not surely die."

"You will be like God."

Therein those three statements lay the deification of man.

First, Eve began to doubt the absolute authority of the Word of God. Did you notice in the dialogue with my facebook friend that he never referenced the Word of God nor did he respond to any of my references? Unless the Bible becomes the basis and authority of our total belief system we will give place to lies, heresies, and doctrines of demons. Satan asked Eve a question that amounted to: "Did God really mean what He said?" That subtle questioning of God's Word then turned into a bold contradiction of it: "You will not surely die." And finally, it ended with a false promise: "You will be like God."

It was when Adam and Eve acted on Satan's subtle suggestion that sin was birthed. Then with sin came sickness, disease, poverty, hatred, strife, suffering, and death. It all began in Lucifer's heart and then was injected into God's first creation before being passed on throughout every generation.

We need to understand the spirit or the heart of man. In the center of every human heart there is a throne. This throne is always occupied by either of two aspirants: God or self. When God is enthroned by the human heart and will, then man is positioned correctly under God's authority. When self is enthroned then God becomes dethroned, and man lives independently of God and becomes his own master, a god unto himself. He establishes the standards of his own happiness and interprets them. This is the deification of man, and it is what Satan offered Eve and what he offers every human being. The Bible correctly calls this self-enthronement godlessness (Rom 1).

The gospel of Jesus Christ is one of self-denial.

"If any man will come after me, let him deny himself, take up his cross, and follow me" (Mat 16:24).

Self-denial is the giving up and surrender of every part of you to God. The real gospel brings man under the total possession of the Lord

Jesus Christ. *Man has a natural aversion to denying himself, and any gospel that caters to this aversion is another gospel.*

Let's look at the account of the rich young ruler and see a demonstration of this aspect of the gospel.

Now as He was going out on the road, one came running, knelt before Him, and asked Him, "Good Teacher, what shall I do that I may inherit eternal life?"

So Jesus said to him, "Why do you call Me good? No one is good but One, that is, God. You know the commandments: 'Do not commit adultery,' 'Do not murder,' 'Do not steal,' 'Do not bear false witness,' 'Do not defraud,' 'Honor your father and your mother.'"

And he answered and said to Him, "Teacher, all these things I have kept from my youth."

Then Jesus, looking at him, loved him, and said to him, "One thing you lack: Go your way, sell whatever you have and give to the poor, and you will have treasure in heaven; and come, take up the cross, and follow Me."

But he was sad at this word, and went away sorrowful, for he had great possessions. (Mark 10:17-22)

This young man was not a casual seeker like so many are today, but was very earnest and sincere. He *ran* to Jesus and *knelt* before Him to inquire of how to obtain this great salvation. Did you notice that when Jesus quoted the Ten Commandments He purposely left out four of them? The commandments He quoted all had to do with the man's relationship to other people while the four He omitted were in respect to his relationship to God. According to Jesus, that is where this man fell short. That is also the reason Jesus did not acknowledge the "Good

Teacher" greeting, but instead pointed the man to God. In other words, Jesus is saying to the rich man, "Since you don't believe I am God why do you call me good? Only God is good." This rich man needed to be made aware that it was his relationship to God that lacked. His riches stood between him and God. In fact, his wealth had become his god. Self was on the throne.

The way to be delivered and set free from the greed and covetousness that was in this man's heart was for him to sell everything he had and give it to the poor. Then in doing so, he would not only have treasure in heaven, but he could then take up his cross and follow Jesus. But the rich man just wouldn't do it. He went away sad. The philosophy of humanism is to make man happy, but the gospel can actually make a man sad until he gets off his throne and surrenders.

Jesus let this man walk away. He did not go after him. He did not change, alter, or modify the gospel for this man as is common done today. He understood that self and God could not jointly rule in this man's heart. Man cannot serve two masters. It was one or the other. There was no negotiation. Today our modern gospel is so different. We have modified the gospel to suit man's love for sin and self.

Chapter 2

THE MODIFICATION OF

THE GOSPEL

"When backsliders, hypocrites, and the half-hearted seeker among us are made to feel comfortable instead of convicted, soothed instead of smitten, pampered instead of pricked, then something is terribly wrong. The holy fire of God is to burn so brightly in the Church that it allows no room for indifference so that hypocrites will not be able to stay and the true seekers will not be able to remain unchanged." - Author

"I marvel that you are turning away so soon from Him who called you in the grace of Christ, to __a different gospel__, which is not another; but there are some who trouble you and want to pervert the gospel of Christ. But even if we, or an angel from heaven, preach any other gospel to you than what we have preached to you, let him be accursed. As we have said before, so now I say again, if anyone preaches any other gospel to you than what you have received, let him be accursed" *(Gal 1:6-9).*

These are the strongest of words penned by the apostle Paul through the inspiration of the Holy Spirit to the Galatian Christians. Twice Paul declares a terrible curse on those who pervert the real gospel of Christ.

One of the great tragedies of the modern Western gospel has been the accentuation of the blessings and benefits of salvation at the exclusion of other components of the cross. There is a very large movement that is sweeping through many churches today that major on life-enhancement, self-help, and self-esteem without hardly ever confronting sin and the works of the flesh. Sadly lacking from this sugar-coated gospel are heart-repentance, holiness, and the empowering grace of God to live in obedience to His demands.

The preachers of this smooth, soft gospel may frequently speak of forgiveness, but rarely do we hear a clear and definitive call for surrender in true repentance. They may even speak of the blood of Christ to cleanse us from our sins, but rarely do we hear of the necessity of that same holy blood to appease the wrath of God against sinners. Frequently we may hear of how Jesus died to make us righteous, but rarely do we use God's holy Law to strip the sinner of his self-righteousness. We may often hear of the need to gain the glories of heaven, but rarely of the need to shun the horrors of hell. At times we may hear of the resurrection of His power (although in many circles that is rare, too), but rarely do we hear of the fellowship of His sufferings. Frequently we hear of the good life we can have now, but rarely do we hear warnings of the judgment to come. And why don't we hear more of the latter? Because we don't want to offend anyone.

The offense of the cross has been virtually removed from our gospel.

What Salvation Army founder William Booth prophesied more than a century ago is increasing at an alarming rate in our day:

"The chief danger of the twentieth century will be:
- *Religion without the Holy Ghost,*
- *Christianity without Christ,*
- *Forgiveness without repentance,*
- *Salvation without regeneration,*
- *Heaven without hell,*
- *And politics without God."*

The twentieth century has already passed, and things don't seem to be improving at all in the twenty-first century.

A new gospel has been produced from the ruling philosophy of the day that says, "If it works, it must be better. If our message adds to our number, if it comforts the people instead of offending them, if it makes them happy, if it keeps them coming to our meetings, and keeps them giving to our causes, then it must be good." The results are what count. This dominating school of thought regards anyone successful as long as they get the job done and accomplish the goals; in this case, growing the church and adding to its membership.

The proponents of this other gospel reason, "More people and more money equal success." It doesn't really matter how they accomplish their goals as long as they do. In this philosophy God becomes a means to an end; a useful God to help them attain the desired success. Others, to sound even more persuasive, may say, "More people means more salvations", but are they really getting saved? Or "More money means a greater propagation of the gospel", but is it the real gospel?

The rich man that went away sorrowfully after Jesus told him to sell his possessions and give the money to the poor would've still been with us today had he heard the modern gospel of goodness, acceptance, and prosperity. Many a popular preacher would've gone after him and negotiated a deal. Instead of a clear call to renounce his materialism, perhaps he could've been more easily convinced to just believe that Jesus was not merely a good teacher, but actually the Son of God. A simple little prayer would've got him in. Maybe he could've been persuaded to give a tithe of his possessions to the ministry instead of selling it all and giving the proceeds to the poor. That would've been much more reasonable and much less offensive to him, and that tithe would really help the church. After all, he had worked hard for his money. Or another popular method employed today would've been to make him an elder and offer him a position in the church and then perhaps his sorrow would be eased and his happiness would return.

This is what we've done with the glorious gospel of our Lord. We've modified it; we've added to it and taken away from it; we've altered it, diluted it, and adapted it to fit the spirit of the age.

Here is the mind-set of those who modify the message of the gospel: "If people are living in sin let's just teach them how to cope. Let's tell them how good God is and how much He loves them no matter how they live or what they've done. If they have an affinity for sinful pleasures then let's not offend them by making mention of that. If they abhor self-denial then let's not talk about that either. Let's just love them without putting any demands or requirements on them. If people want to be entertained then let's entertain them. Then our message will be even more appealing to them. Let's meet everyone where they're at. We'll use short, non-confronting sermons and humorous skits and dramas in a friendly way to spark their interest. Gradually they will come around, and God's love will change them."

This "new" mind-set has spawned a "new" gospel that is flourishing. Mega churches are being grown from this gospel in virtually every major city in America and other nations as well. Pastors are the CEO's of these churches that are being managed like corporations. Deceitful workers are transforming themselves into the apostles of Christ who glory in their flesh, their growth, their numbers, and their influence, while deceiving so many others. These men boast of their new gospel and methods of reaching people while daring to criticize the old-fashioned gospel as being out of date and out of style and not meeting today's needs.

The new preachers of this new gospel preach love, but it's a love that never rebukes, corrects, or trains. They mention the name of Jesus, but it's another Jesus that they have formed in their own image according to the godless pop culture around them. They talk about a loving heavenly Father, but know nothing of God being an All Consuming Fire. While emphasizing the goodness of God they completely avoid warnings of His severity (Rom 11:22).

If a man is ambitious, has strong leadership skills, a warming charismatic personality, and he knows how to employ the right formula and new methods, he can grow a church almost overnight, especially by preaching a non-confronting, non-convicting gospel and giving people what their itching ears want to hear. At the core of these new preachers' ambition, however, is an insatiable desire for an honored reputation and an unsanctified drive for quick growth and quick results that would give them greater power and influence.

Men find great fulfillment in significance so any hook with the bait of power and success dangling from it is an easy temptation. Yet we must realize that some of the greatest failures by human standards are God's greatest successes. God's measuring gauge and standard of success is so different than man's.

Noah would be the classic example of a great failure today. His message and ministry spanned 120 years, but produced no converts outside of his own family. He was an excellent carpenter and ship builder, but as a preacher he failed and didn't get the job done: No numbers, no following, and no influence. The gospel he preached and the methods he used produced nothing. But the Bible speaks of him in lofty terms calling him a preacher of righteousness (2 Pet 2:5), obedient (Gen 6:22, 7:5), and perfect (blameless, having integrity).

"This is the genealogy of Noah. Noah was a just man, perfect in his generations. Noah walked with God" (Gen 6:9).

"Then the LORD said to Noah, "Come into the ark, you and all your household, because I have seen that <u>you are righteous before Me in this generation</u>" (Gen 7:1).

What would you rather have written on your tombstone - the accolades of men that were lies, or the testimony of God that remains forever true? What do you want your epitaph to say? Do you want to be honored by earth or by heaven? How do you want to be remembered?

Where did we get the idea that if the size of churches and ministries are not numerically large, do not grow fast, or do not grow at all, and do not meet man's approval they are automatically counted as failures? From whence comes this persuasion?

By using the right formula and Madison Avenue tactics almost anyone can draw a crowd and build a church today. Add to that, an entertainment, socially-adapted, fun-based "gospel" message and people will come. Then word will spread and more people will come.

Here's an example I heard the late David Wilkerson share years ago: During one Sunday night gathering in a seeker-friendly church where thousands attended, the pastor got up and said: "This is a fun night, a David Letterman night." Then the youth pastor came out and did a monologue as David Letterman. He showed 10 of the most boring things teenagers do during preaching. Three of the ten were throwing spitballs, yawning, and picking their noses. The people in attendance went wild with laughter and great applause. As the church service was closing the pastor shamelessly announced, "We're not here to offend anyone, but to make church comfortable for everybody."

How many people do you think would remain in that church if the pastor changed his philosophy and suddenly began preaching a strong anti-sin, anti-worldliness, cross-bearing, Jesus exalting repentance message? I'll tell you exactly what would happen. It would cause a church split. Some would be offended and leave. Others would be convicted and repent. But what would we rather have: 1000 false converts or 100 true ones? The way you win people is the way you keep them. If you win them with entertainment you're going to have to entertain them to keep them. If you win them with a soft gospel you're going to have to continue to feed them a soft gospel to keep them. Falsehood, half-truths, and compromise will beget more of the same. A defective gospel produces defective converts.

I heard a television preacher say that in one mega church he spoke at he discovered that 60 couples were living together out of wedlock. Not one of them was legally married. The reason given: None of them thought it was wrong. How shocking! Here's the question I have: What kind of message were the pastors of that church preaching? Obviously a very defective one. The fruit of a false gospel is false converts. Faith without works is always dead.

The Church today is full of false converts who have never been searched out and convicted of their sins. They come to church meetings, they sing church songs, they talk the church language, and hear church sermons, but they live like the world. Their lifestyles are in contradiction to the Word of God. One man said, "I know I shouldn't be shacking up with my girlfriend, but I believe in Jesus and He knows my heart." The Bible says that the demons also believe and tremble (Jam 2:19). In other words, the demons believe and fear God more than those like this man who say they believe, but have no works or corresponding lifestyle to prove their faith (that is the context of Jam 2:14-18).

When you leave certain components of the cross out of the gospel you open a large door for the sinner and the half-hearted seeker to feel comfortable in their sins and in their worldly lifestyle. And when that becomes the norm or status quo in a church, deception spreads like a cancer. A false or an incomplete gospel establishes an atmosphere of deception. People are being errantly taught that all you need to do to be saved is to acknowledge your belief in Jesus, pray a little prayer, and you're in. Nothing is ever said before or after salvation about true heart-repentance, surrendering your life - losing it to gain it, following Jesus in whole-hearted obedience, and loving Him above all others.

I'd like to share another story that will serve as one more example of a deceived people, who due to *not* hearing the whole counsel of God had become comfortable in their sinful lifestyle. This true account does not end well and serves to show the tragic consequences of the failure to preach the real gospel.

Years ago I took a Bible school group of 10 students to a church in a large city in America. God led me to preach a very strong message on repentance. As I was giving the altar call people began to come forward. Before I could instruct them, however, the pastor stepped in and brought the entire service to a halt. He accused me of being hard and defended himself and his people, saying that they were all just as saved as I or anyone else was. He then asked me to come to his office and further reprimanded me for my message. The Lord told me to keep my mouth shut and not say anything. This pastor then cancelled the rest of the meetings we were to have in his church, and also called all the other churches in the area that we were scheduled to minister in and convinced the pastors of those churches to cancel the remainder of our meetings as well.

Within a day or two of that particular meeting I received a vision from the Lord to explain what had happened in that church. In the vision he showed me a large snake all coiled up on top of a mound of sand. Then he showed me cocking my right arm back and firing a rock that hit him right between the eyes. Suddenly that snake uncoiled, raised up his ugly head, and hissed loudly while shaking violently and scattering sand everywhere. His secure stronghold had been threatened. The Lord showed me that there were serious sin issues in that church beginning with the pastor himself, and the message I preached shook and unsettled everything.

Sometime later a brother whom we found favor with from this hosting church wrote me at my request to let me know what transpired in that church over the next several years. Within two years the children's pastor was charged with child molestation. Think of the damage done to those children. Then the pastor's daughter was caught having an affair with her boss. Her husband died a couple of years after that. This adulteress woman has a beautiful daughter who loves Jesus, but to this day she enjoys no relationship with her. This is the rotten fruit of sin. That's not all, though. A few years later the host pastor, who was responsible for virtually kicking us out of town, suddenly fell dead of a massive heart attack on a Sunday morning right before a service. Another pastor, who had cancelled our meetings because the host pastor encouraged him to, was also caught in adultery and lost his church. It turns out this other pastor only cancelled our meetings because the host pastor was the biggest financial contributor of his television ministry.

All these casualties happened because people were made to feel comfortable in their sin; because no one preached the confrontational aspects of the gospel. Judgment caught up with people in this church because they were not willing to judge themselves. Think about that.

Evil and wickedness were actually strengthened because preachers failed to stand in the counsel of the Lord and speak His words.

"They strengthen also the hands of evildoers, that none returns from his wickedness...But if they had stood in my counsel, and had

caused my people to hear my words, then they should have turned them from their evil way, and from the evil of their doings" (Jer 23: 14, 22).

Somehow people think it is mean-spirited and even condemning to preach the cross and a confrontational gospel that deals with sin and worldliness and calls people to repentance, when actually it is the mercy of God and His saving grace to do so.

The real life examples I listed above are a direct result of a failure to preach the real gospel and to warn people of impending judgment and the consequences of sin. Ministers will be held accountable for not preaching the full counsel of God. God hates deception because it eventually destroys people, brings judgment upon them, and is eternally fatal. Notice again these extremely strong words from the Amplified version of the Bible and the very heavy indictment given to those who preach another gospel:

"But even if we or an angel from heaven should preach to you a gospel contrary to and different from that which we preached to you, let him be accursed (anathema, devoted to destruction, doomed to eternal punishment)! As we said before, so I now say again: If anyone is preaching to you a gospel different from or contrary to that which you received [from us], let him be accursed (anathema, devoted to destruction, doomed to eternal punishment)" (Gal 1:8-9 Amp)!

Do we really believe that such a horrific curse pronounced on false preachers of a false gospel is in the Bible? Does this really mean what it says? Whenever something is repeated in the same context of Scripture we better pay very close attention to it and understand God's heart in the matter. His anger and severity with all those who preach another gospel is glaringly evident here. Why is this most damning terminology used to devote and doom men to destruction and eternal punishment?

I'll tell you why: Because a false gospel deceives and damns souls. It insults the precious blood of Christ and the agony and sacrifice He made for the sin of the world. It takes away the glory from the redemptive work of Jesus. It stains and contaminates the glorious bride of Christ. And in this context, it threatened to cause these young Galatian converts to depart from Christ and the real faith.

"Whoever causes one of these little ones who believe in Me to sin, it would be better for him if a millstone were hung around his neck, and he were drowned in the depth of the sea" (Mat 18:6).

I don't want the blood of sinners on my hands because of a failure to preach the real Biblical gospel. Paul preached in order to present every man perfect in Christ Jesus (Col 1:28). May we do the same and save our necks and those who hear us.

Chapter 3

THE OFFENSE OF THE CROSS

"I'd rather offend man and please God than please man and offend God. Better to offend man and God be for you, than offend God and have Him against you." Author

"And I, brethren, if I still preach circumcision, why do I still suffer persecution? Then the offense of the cross has ceased" (Gal 5:11).

"As many as desire to make a good showing in the flesh, these would compel you to be circumcised, only that they may not suffer persecution for the cross of Christ. For not even those who are circumcised keep the law, but they desire to have you circumcised that they may boast in your flesh. But God forbid that I should boast except in the cross of our Lord Jesus Christ, by whom the world has been crucified to me, and I to the world" (Gal 6:12-14).

Have you ever wondered why there is little persecution in the West for preaching the gospel? Have you ever wondered why there is also much deception in the West? And why is there not more of a sharp line of distinction between the Church and the world? The answer to all these questions is probably the same. The real gospel of the cross of Christ has not been preached nor practiced. The offensiveness of the cross has been taken away.

Today you will rarely find preachers who are preaching circumcision as a means of salvation, but to avoid persecution, many water-down the message of the cross, altering it and adapting it to make it less offensive and more acceptable to the masses. By removing the offense of the cross they remove the heart and foundation of the gospel.

The offense of the cross arises chiefly from the fact that it condemns every other way of salvation. The cross condemns justification by any system of works. The cross opposes all human wisdom, human ability, and human merit. The cross opposes all self-righteousness, self-glorification, and self-seeking.

The cross of our Lord Jesus Christ is an offense to every person who enjoys sinning. Many want to have Jesus without forsaking their sin. Many want to have Jesus without forsaking the world. Many want to have Jesus while continuing to seek their own will. Many exalt their own religion whether it is Islam, Buddhism, Hinduism, or any other kind of 'ism above Jesus, or they add Jesus to it. Many want to hang on to their man-made traditions, denominational doctrines, and humanistic philosophies that are contrary to the gospel. The cross of Christ confronts all these things.

The way to destruction is broad and appealing to multitudes, but the way to eternal life is narrow and traveled by few (Mat 7:13-14). The cross of Jesus Christ is the narrow way.

Any gospel that proclaims a salvation without the cross is "another" gospel. It is sad to see how a great number of preachers today have bypassed or done away with the preaching of the cross of Jesus Christ. It is even possible to refer to the historical Jesus and preach about the crucifixion, describing the sufferings of Christ in strikingly vivid detail, as many preachers do, for example on Easter, and still miss the main points of the cross. If there is no confrontation of man's sinful nature, evil deeds, and rebellion that brings him to a crisis, then it is not the cross of Christ.

"Verily, verily, I say unto you, He that enters not by the door into the sheepfold, but climbs up some other way, the same is a thief and a robber" (John 10:1).

When Jesus says, "I am the way" and "I am the door," He is speaking of the cross. He is saying, "You cannot be saved, you cannot enter the kingdom, you cannot inherit eternal life unless you enter by way of the cross. Anyone who tells you any differently is a thief and a robber."

The thief and the robber will tell you repentance is not necessary. They say that Jesus has paid for all your sins, and you just need to accept the payment. They say all you have to do is believe. They say you don't need to worry about your sins because Jesus took care of the sin problem. They say that God loves you just the way you are. Now I'm not saying there isn't any truth in these statements, but where is the offense in it? Satan will not deceive with lies. He will deceive with truth that has a lie attached to it. There is an Arabic proverb that says: "All liars tell the truth."

I'm not saying that you should purposely try to be offensive. Nowhere in the New Testament did the apostles use fleshly means to preach the gospel in order to cause *unnecessary* offense to people. On the contrary, Paul and the other apostles would go out of their way to avoid putting stumbling blocks to the gospel in front of people. Paul made sure his actions did not drive people away from the gospel. He was always loving and respectful, even denying himself certain liberties to win people to Christ. *"I am made all things to all men, that I might by all means save some" (1 Cor 9:22).* He did all this without compromising the gospel. We are to pursue peace with all men (free of offense) without compromising the message of the cross which is holiness (and causes offense).

"Pursue peace with all people, and holiness, without which no one will see the Lord" (Heb 12:14).

Although we are to avoid being unnecessarily offensive to people, we must realize that if we are never persecuted, or the gospel we preach never offends anyone, it strongly suggests we are not preaching the message of the cross.

I have a friend named Jim in my home town that I've been a witness of the gospel to for many months now. At first he was confused about Christianity to such a degree that he wasn't even sure who Jesus was. He is highly intellectual and couldn't see how God could make Jesus the only way to salvation. He would reason, "How could God allow good human beings who have another religion to perish and go to hell?" I talked to him several times and eventually asked him to read the gospel of John so that he could see that the loopholes he was trying to find in the person of Jesus Christ and the gospel just aren't there.

Finally, the light came on and he began to understand that there was no other way to God except through Jesus. Still, he struggled with the need to change his lifestyle saying things like, "Nothing is broken in my life. Nothing needs fixing." He believed that the guiding principle of his life to do good to others was enough. In other words, although he now believed that Jesus was the Son of God, that He shed His blood for his sins, that He was raised from the dead, he was not yet convicted of his sins. What if I had told Jim: "Don't worry about your sins, Jim. Jesus paid for it all. Just receive God's payment and confess Jesus, and you'll be saved."

I'll tell you what would've happened. By ministering a false comfort to him and rushing him to a decision to pray a prayer of salvation when conviction wasn't working, deception would've been birthed in his life. He would've believed he was saved without really being saved.

This is what has been done with multitudes of sinners everywhere, and that is the key reason why such a small percentage of them continue to walk with the Lord and bear fruit after supposedly receiving Jesus. We think we can bypass the cross and use other methods to bring people to salvation, and in so doing we become guilty of preaching another gospel and leaving so many in deception.

The more I talked to Jim the more I began to locate the root of his problem. He felt he would be unhappy with a different lifestyle than the one he has now. His current lifestyle includes regular Friday or Saturday night parties at his house where he and his friends drink booze and carry on until the wee hours of the morning. That's what the Holy Spirit was pressing and putting his finger on. So now there was conviction, but Jim was resisting the Holy Spirit in the process. It was all an issue of repentance and surrender. To this day I continue to meet with him and one other new convert in a Bible study, which Jim actually enjoys, but he has not yet come to salvation.

You see, the sinner believes that there can be no real enjoyment in life if he stops sinning. He does not seem to realize that the person who has repented has no desire to sin. The grace of God changes a person's desires and empowers him to live for Christ. It is an inward transformation. That's the miracle of salvation. I dare to say that if the desire to sin is still in the heart of a professing Christian then he has not yet tasted of the real salvation. New life has not yet begun. Regeneration has not taken place. Listen to the voice of one of the great revivalists of the past:

"Christianity does not make the believer unhappy by keeping him away from the sinful things he loved because the believer has changed his opinion on those things." Charles G. Finney

41

Finney defined repentance as a change of the ultimate preference or choice of the soul and of action. He taught that repentance is a change of will, feeling, and of life in respect toward God. Finney believed that true repentance involves more of the person's will and conscience than his natural feelings. Feelings are involuntary and have no moral character except what they derive from the action and the will. He would admonish sinners to submit and commit their entire being to God at once, obey their conscience, and the feelings would soon follow. God requires you to will right.

Let me make one thing clear. When I speak of the will I am not speaking of "will power" or a heavy self-effort that puts an emphasis on trying harder, committing more, quitting all your sins and then coming to Jesus. That's not the gospel either. That is legalism and a works-based gospel no different than circumcision was under the Law, and it leaves the sinner frustrated and without grace and hope. Repentance is something the Holy Spirit works in your heart. You cannot generate your own repentance. Your responsibility is to respond to His working. God provides the grace, but you still have to cooperate with Him. Cooperation is simply responding to God's ability. Notice what the Holy Spirit has come to do:

"Nevertheless I tell you the truth. It is to your advantage that I go away; for if I do not go away, the Helper will not come to you; but if I depart, I will send Him to you. And when He has come, He will convict the world of sin, and of righteousness, and of judgment: of sin, because they do not believe in Me; of righteousness, because I go to My Father and you see Me no more; of judgment, because the ruler of this world is judged" (John 16:7-11).

One of the chief functions of the mighty Holy Spirit is to convict the world of sin, righteousness, and judgment. There can be no repentance without conviction. The power to produce a change of heart does not come from a strong will, self-effort, or reform, but from the Holy Spirit prompting the sinner to submit his will. It is purely a supernatural work of grace from conviction to repentance to the manifest fruit of repentance in the person's behavior and conduct. Many people may even acknowledge their sin, respond to the call to repent, but then they resist the Holy Spirit in the process as He follows through in conjunction with the Word of God to bring about corresponding actions in their lives. That's the reason why many sinners often pray for salvation, but never bear any fruit of a changed life. Still others respond to the call to repent, but try and produce a change of heart and life in their own strength.

The culmination of true repentance is a turning from sin toward God, and then exercising your faith toward the Lord Jesus Christ. It is impossible to place your faith and complete trust in Jesus Christ for salvation without turning away from your sins in repentance. Anything short of this is not Biblical salvation. That is the message that Jesus and Paul both preached.

"Now after John was put in prison, Jesus came to Galilee, preaching the gospel of the kingdom of God, and saying, 'The time is fulfilled, and the kingdom of God is at hand. Repent, and believe in the gospel'" (Mk 1:14-15).

"Testifying to Jews, and also to Greeks, repentance toward God and faith toward our Lord Jesus Christ" (Acts 20:21).

I've read books written by ministers implying that repentance is no longer necessary under the New Covenant. Others would not go so far as to make such foolish claims, but erred the same way by making light of repentance or never mentioning it at all. They loudly proclaim all that is needed for salvation is faith in the finished work of Christ while downplaying repentance as if it is somehow a dirty word. These ministers will expound on this by quoting certain scriptures that highlight the element of faith in salvation, based purely on grace without works, which of course is absolutely true, and should always be emphasized, but they leave out other aspects of salvation and the cross. They emphasize such scriptures as Paul and Silas' response to only "believe" when they were asked by the Philippian jailer, "What must I do to be saved?" (Acts 16:31), the "believe and confess" component in Rom 10:9-10, and the "believe" of John 3:16 (John's gospel alone has many such references), but often isolate these from such scriptures as, Acts 2:38, Acts 3:19, Acts 5:31 and a host of others where repentance is highlighted. We need to understand that repentance is a part of the great commission and what Jesus told us to preach (Lk 24:47).

Are repentance and faith polar opposites? Are they at odds with one another? Is it two different coins we are playing with, or two sides of the same coin? Has the professing Christian who is shacking up with his girlfriend and says: "I know I'm not living right, but I believe in Jesus and he knows my heart,"- really come to repentance? Is that kind of belief in Jesus enough to get him in? Did Christ die so we could continue living in sin? Is that what these following verses say?

"Knowing this, that our old man was crucified with Him, that the body of sin might be done away with, that we should no longer be slaves of sin" (Rom 6:6).

"But God be thanked that though you were slaves of sin, yet you obeyed from the heart that form of doctrine to which you were delivered. And having been set free from sin, you became slaves of righteousness" (Rom 6:17-18).

"Who Himself bore our sins in His own body on the tree, that we, having died to sins, might live for righteousness—by whose stripes you were healed" (1 Pet 2:24).

44

Here's the problem with the modern salvation doctrine: It's unsound because it's unbalanced. Preachers today are infamous for beating their pet hobby horse into the ground. They take isolated scriptures or one ingredient of the gospel of salvation or any other topic, and make an entire doctrine out of it. For example, they've done that with the word "believe" or faith. As important as faith is to our salvation and Christian walk, it is only one ingredient of salvation and our walk with God. We've already seen that without repentance toward God, faith toward the Lord Jesus Christ cannot be exercised (Acts 20:21). Furthermore, without grace there is no saving faith (Eph 2:8). Without works and obedience, faith is dead (Jam 2:17, 24). Without hope, faith has no substance (Heb 11:1). Without love, faith does not work (Gal 5:6). So as you can see, faith never stands on its own, but is a part of a sum of other attributes that bring balance to the Scriptures.

From Genesis to Revelation the Bible is an integrated whole and represents the complete counsel of God. *"Therefore I testify to you this day that I am innocent of the blood of all men. For I have not shunned to declare to you the whole counsel of God" (Acts 20:26-27).* Paul was innocent of the blood of all men because he declared the whole counsel of God. This implies that anyone who has failed to declare the whole counsel of God is guilty in some way of the blood of men. Contrary to popular opinion, the Bible does not teach that faith is the *only* requirement for salvation. Actually there are a number of scriptures that point to other aspects of the gospel by which a person is saved. Here are some:

1. Grace (Eph 2:8)

2. Repentance (Lk 13:3, 5)

3. Believe and confess Jesus as Lord (Rom 10:9)

4. Belief and baptism (Mk 16:16)

45

5. Calling on the Lord (Acts 2:21)

6. Holiness (Heb 12:14)

7. Obedience (Heb 5:9)

8. Endurance (Mat 24:13)

Unlike many modern day preachers who repeatedly say that belief in Jesus with a very minimal level of commitment is all that is required to be saved, all these ingredients have a part to play in our salvation. "All you need to do to be guaranteed a place in heaven is just believe", seems to be the common dirge of the hour. Repentance doesn't matter. Obedience doesn't matter. Holiness doesn't matter. I'm certainly not minimizing the importance of faith and believing, but in our day the word "believe" has been defined as mental ascent or agreement and applied in a loose sort of way. In other words, just believe that Jesus exists. Just believe that Jesus died for your sins. Just receive His forgiveness. This is the Western gospel that is heard in our pulpits, on the airwaves, taught in our Bible schools and seminaries, and read in our contemporary Christian books and magazines. The offense of the cross has been removed to make the gospel more palatable to the masses, and as a result, has lulled our churches into a false sense of security.

This is exactly why the preaching of the cross must be restored to our gospel and accompanied by a call to repentance and evidenced by the fruit of obedience. Justification by faith must be forever joined to a life of holiness and sanctification. The cross is a place of death to sin and our old self, while the resurrection is a birth of newness of life. There can be no resurrection and a newness of life without death. It's much easier on a person's pride if we can just skip over the offense of the cross and move right into the resurrection. It is much more appealing and an easier "sell" to speak of the power of a new life and the peace, joy, and blessings you will experience. It's much more affirming to build up a man than to tear him down. But our union with Christ is first at the cross in His death, then in His burial, resurrection, ascension, and His seating at the right hand of God (Rom 6:3-4, Eph 2:6).

"For I determined not to know anything among you except Jesus Christ and Him crucified" (1 Cor 2:2).

The entire process of salvation from conversion to discipleship can be very humiliating. The cross is not only central to salvation, but also to authentic Christian living. Jesus calls for a total forsaking of our own lives (Mat 16:24-25, Lk 16:33). He demands a complete allegiance to His will (Mat 6:24). He requires loyalty to Him even above your closest family ties (Mat 10:37, Lk 14:26).There is a crisis at the cross. There is a confrontation and a subsequent conflict between flesh and spirit. We've skirted these issues because we want to avoid the offense and escape the persecution that comes with it. We want people to feel accepted and esteemed before they die at the cross. The plan of salvation will not work by short-cutting the death process. The sinner who comes to the cross must be prepared to die. There is no negotiating. There are no options. At the cross we die to our sins and no longer live for ourselves.

"And He died for all, that those who live should live no longer for themselves, but for Him who died for them and rose again" (2 Cor 5:15).

"And those who are Christ's have crucified the flesh with its passions and desires" (Gal 5:24).

Besides the Biblical references already mentioned, what kind of gospel did Jesus preach? Did His message ever cause offense? Did it shatter people's religiosity and upset their man-made traditions? What example did Jesus leave us?

When Jesus performed miracles, healed the sick, and fed the multitudes people would flock to Him (John 6:2, 26), but often their motives were wrong. They didn't follow Jesus because they wanted to honor Him for His miraculous power or because they wanted to hear the wisdom and truth of His words, but because they *ate the loaves and were filled*. As is common today, the multitudes followed Jesus for the benefits of what He could do for them and what He could give them. So what did Jesus do with these kinds of people? His custom was to sift the crowds by preaching messages and speaking words, often in parables, that would expose people's impure motives, pride, and cut through their false pretenses.

For example, in John 6 He began to expound on who He was, the true Bread which came down from heaven, saying that people must eat of His flesh and drink of His blood to have eternal life. These sayings were hard to receive and actually sounded like some kind of cannibalism. The Jews did not even eat pork and ham much less human flesh. This offended the Jews and also His disciples. Not only was Jesus prophesying of the death He would soon die, but also of the necessity of His followers to identify with Him. When Jesus spoke of the cost of following Him many left, and this is the pattern throughout the gospels. *Therein lay a great scriptural principle: The closer you get to the cross the less people there are.*

"Then Jesus said to them, "Most assuredly, I say to you, unless you eat the flesh of the Son of Man and drink His blood, you have no life in you. Whoever eats My flesh and drinks My blood has eternal life, and I will raise him up at the last day" (John 6:53-54).

"Therefore many of His disciples, when they heard this, said, 'This is a hard saying; who can understand it?' When Jesus knew in Himself that His disciples complained about this, He said to them, "Does this offend you? What then if you should see the Son of Man ascend where He was before? It is the Spirit who gives life; the flesh profits nothing. The words that I speak to you are spirit, and they are life. But there are some of you who do not believe." For Jesus knew from the beginning who they were who did not believe, and who would betray Him. And He said, "Therefore I have said to you that no one can come to Me unless it has been granted to him by My Father. From that time many of His disciples went back and walked with Him no more" (John 6:61-66).

Many of Jesus' own disciples were offended at His hard sayings and left Him. What we've done today is eliminate the hard sayings of the gospel to avoid offense in order to conjure up results and increase our numbers. Jesus, however, did quite the opposite. Often He would preach in such a way so as to make it difficult for naturally-minded, self-seeking people to follow Him. We've already seen that He did this with the rich young ruler when Jesus told him to sell everything he possessed, give to the poor, and then follow Him. Jesus sifted the crowds for two basic reasons:

1) He knew that no man could even come to Him except the Father draw him (John 6:65). He knew also that those whom the heavenly Father had given Him would follow Him and no man would be able to snatch them out of His hand (John 10:27-29).

2) He also knew that the kingdom of God would be stronger and the purity of the Church preserved with a few whole-hearted followers than a multitude of self-centered people who appear to follow Jesus outwardly but whose motives were not pure.

The hard sayings of Jesus would chase away the hypocrites and self-seekers while drawing the true disciples closer. True disciples, because they are spiritually minded, love hard truth and embrace the offense of the cross. While the hard sayings of Jesus offends false followers still today, the meat and substance of Jesus' words is truly food that edifies and strengthens true followers.

Years ago I heard a story about the Communist KGB Russian police breaking into an underground church meeting and commanding the believers there to renounce Jesus or be shot. A number of them did so and were released. Then the KGB removed their uniforms revealing their true identity as fellow believers in disguise. They embraced the remaining believers and counted them as true followers. This is what Jesus also did.

Some people will follow Jesus for awhile outwardly, but soon draw back when they are offended. This is proof that they were not true followers to begin with. The same is true today. Many who profess Christ outwardly possess no corresponding lifestyle as evidence of grace's reality in their lives.

Let us never forget that the real gospel causes offense and persecution. The world's antichrist system currently under the sway of the wicked one (1 John 5:19) is in direct opposition to the message of the cross. The cross is against everything the world stands for; the lust of the flesh, the lust of the eyes, and the pride of life (1 John 2:16). Let us also remember that it was the spirit of the world working through the hard-hearted Jews that killed Jesus, the sinless Son of God. That is what the evil nature of man is capable of, and that is also what the cross has bridged.

Besides Jesus, the original apostles suffered great persecution and most of them were also martyred for preaching the same message.

Additionally, millions of other Christians have been either killed or have suffered persecution throughout the centuries for preaching the real gospel.

Suffering persecution is a part of the gospel. Jesus said the world will hate you and persecute you (John 15:18-20), and families will be divided (Luke 12:51-53) because of Jesus and the gospel. In Matthew 10:17-22 He said to His disciples that men would deliver them up to councils, scourge them in their synagogues, family members would put other family members to death, and all men would hate them because of the gospel.

The book of Acts is also full of the exploits of the apostles and the early Church, but it is also full of the persecutions they suffered. Threatenings, imprisonments, beatings, stonings, deaths, riots, and uproars were frequent and all a part of preaching the gospel, but so were salvations, miracles, deliverances, and revivals. This is the nature of our gospel and one that needs to be desperately restored.

"And blessed is he who is not offended because of Me" (Luke 7:23).

Chapter 4

THE JUDICIAL ASPECT OF THE CROSS

"The Most Beloved Son and the Darling of heaven died a criminal's death for crimes He did not do; imagine the Holy Creator becoming the Slaughtered Lamb, so that His life could flow to me and you." Author

"For the law of the Spirit of life in Christ Jesus has made me free from the law of sin and death" (Rom 8:1).

"He who justifies the wicked, and he who condemns the just, both of them are an abomination to God" (Proverbs 17:15).

"He is the Rock, His work is perfect; For all His ways are justice, A God of truth and without injustice; Righteous and upright is He" (Deut 32:4).

Many people, even Christians, do not fully understand why Jesus Christ, the Son of God, had to die. Why the cross? Why the blood? How is it that salvation can come through the blood of a man's death on a cross?

Unless you understand God's holy and just nature and the laws He has set in motion, and their purpose, you will not grasp the true meaning of the cross of Jesus Christ. One of the first laws God established back in the garden of Eden was the law of sin and death.

"And the LORD God commanded the man, saying, "Of every tree of the garden you may freely eat; but of the tree of the knowledge of good

and evil you shall not eat, for in the day that you eat of it you shall surely die" (Gen 2:16-17).

"For the wages of sin is death..." (Rom 6:23).

God told Adam that sin must be paid for or punished with death. Just as every lawbreaker and criminal in society must be sentenced in a court of law and punished so every sinner must suffer the penalty for their sin. This is the first law given to man called *"the law of sin and death"* (Rom 8:2). Sin is breaking God's law (1 John 3:4), and it causes a three-fold separation:

1. Spiritual death (separation from God)

2. Physical death (spirit separated from body)

3. Eternal death or the second death (eternal separation from God)

Sin is the greatest problem and curse known to the human race and cannot be taken lightly because it separates man from God (Isa 59:2) and produces death. The best way to illustrate this would be to break off a healthy branch from a tree. The branch may look alive for awhile, but it is dead because it has been cut off from its life source. When Adam and Eve sinned they were separated from the living God, their Creator, and their Life Source. Immediately they died spiritually, and then they began to die physically. And if God had not devised a plan of rescue and redemption, man's eternal destiny would've been the lake of fire, or what the Bible calls the second death (Rev 20:14-15).

The entire human race was infected with Adam's sinful nature, even babies. That's why little children are naturally selfish and hurtful while being good and kind requires effort and struggle. When children reach the age of accountability (usually between the ages of 9-11) God holds them responsible for their sin. Some people may defend their innocence and say, "It's not my fault I was born this way." Again, when you cut a branch off from a tree, regardless of how large the branch is, all the twigs coming from that branch are dead. If a river's source is contaminated all the water in that river is contaminated. If the water in a well is contaminated, every bucket drawn from it is also contaminated. If a reservoir or a water tank is contaminated all the drinking water flowing through pipes into people's homes in that community is contaminated. In the same way, sin and death have been passed on to all of Adam's descendants and contaminated every single one of them. This is tragic, but nevertheless true.

"Therefore, just as through one man sin entered the world, and death through sin, and thus death spread to all men, because all sinned" (Rom 5:12).

"Behold, I was brought forth in iniquity, and in sin my mother conceived me" (Ps 51:5).

"The wicked are estranged from the womb; they go astray as soon as they are born, speaking lies" (Ps 58:3).

The law of sin and death is just that: It is GOD'S LAW! And His law demands that every act of rebellion and disobedience be punished with death. According to God's standard of justice, the entire human race deserves the death penalty (Rom 3:23). It is because of God's holy and just nature that He must uphold and execute this law. What would you think of a judge who did not uphold the law?

Parents, if your virgin daughter was brutally raped what would you think of a judge who failed to punish the guilty offender? He would be an unjust judge. Now suppose as the courtroom rises expecting to hear the judge pronounce a death sentence, or life in prison on the guilty rapist, but instead all who are gathered in the courtroom hear the judge say these words: "I've done some research on you and I've discovered that you have given much to charity, you've also invested much time in community service, and I can tell you are a praying man by how you've been handling those beads. Very impressive! This is a tough call, but your good works outweigh your bad works. I'm going to grant you mercy and pardon. You are released and free to enter society again." The judge then strikes the gavel as the entire courtroom stands in shock. Was it really mercy this judge extended to the guilty, or was it the gravest of injustices?

Such a scenario is unheard of in today's court system. Whether or not the criminal's good works outweigh his bad does not sway the guilty verdict. If such a system does not hold up in an earthly courtroom, would it hold up in a heavenly one? Do you think that a man's sense of justice is greater than God's? Yet people seem to think that God's mercy will automatically forgive man's sin and allow all guilty sinners entrance into heaven. Such an unscriptural mercy does not exist. How strange that man should possess such a strong, innate sense of justice while somehow believing that God, the faithful and righteous judge of all the earth, does not!

God cannot disregard His own laws. When it comes to sin God can never set aside justice to show mercy. The soul that sins must die (Ez 18:20), and yet God has no pleasure in the death of the wicked (Ez 33:11). So the question is: Is there a basis by which God can maintain His justice while still extending mercy to the sinner? That is the issue.

Anyone who suggests that God can show mercy while foregoing justice is ignoring His holy nature and His law of sin and death. What kind of faith could we have in a Creator who ignores the laws He Himself has established thus contradicting His own holy and righteous character? What kind of hope and trust could we exercise toward a god like that who is whimsical, unpredictable, and fickle?

God's justice and mercy are not at odds with each other, but are always in perfect balance. Forgiveness of sins is not a simple matter for a holy God. God cannot show mercy to a sinner without the sinner's transgressions being punished and satisfied by the claims of justice. This perfect and infinitely holy Judge cannot say: "It's okay that you sinned. Forget about it. I forgive you." Or, "Because of my love I won't judge you." Nor would God say: "I don't love you anymore because you sinned." His love and judgment do not contradict each other. God loves sinners, and desires that none perish (2 Pet 3:9), but He must still execute judgment and punishment on their sin. The question again rephrased is this: How can a holy and righteous God extend mercy toward a guilty sinner while still upholding His justice? This was the dilemma that Adam's sin produced, and as we will see, it was one of the first lessons God taught His first creation.

When Adam and Eve sinned they became conscious of their shame and nakedness. Filled now with fear, they hid themselves from God, and then made clothing out of fig leaves to cover their nakedness. God rejected their self-efforts to solve their sin problem (as He does today), and instead He provided the first animal sacrifice ever in order to cover Adam and Eve's sin and shame. God would also provide the final sacrifice for sin thousands of years later in the person of His Son Jesus Christ. In essence, that animal became a substitutionary sacrifice for Adam's sin. This was another law God instituted called the *law of sacrifice*.

"Then the LORD God made clothes out of animal skins for the man and his wife" (Gen 3:21 CEV).

This law of sacrifice taught Adam and Eve that it takes the death of an innocent animal and shed blood to satisfy God's justice and to nullify the penalty for man's sin. A life must be substituted for another life. Only the law of sacrifice could negate the law of sin and death.

Adam and Eve's first offspring, Cain and Abel, were taught this same lesson by their parents, but only Abel believed it by offering to God an innocent lamb while Cain offered up an assortment of fruits and vegetables he had worked so hard to harvest. Yet God, in the same way He had rejected Adam and Eve's self-efforts to cover their sin and shame with fig leaves, rejected Cain's offering while respecting Abel's (Gen 4:1-5). Through Abel's faith he pleased God by submitting to God's law of sacrifice while Cain attempted to come to God on his own terms (Heb 11:4, 6). Although sin's effects were a part of both Cain and Abel's character, because of God's love and desire to have a relationship with them, He established this law of sacrifice to make atonement for their sin since it is man's sin that separates him from God.

"For the life of the flesh is in the blood, and I have given it to you upon the altar to make atonement for your souls; for it is the blood that makes atonement for the soul" (Lev 17:11 NKJ).

"Life is in the blood, and I have given you the blood of animals to sacrifice in place of your own" (Lev 17:11 CEV).

It was through the sacrifice of an unblemished animal that God punished sin without punishing the sinner. Worshippers were instructed to select a healthy animal such as a lamb, a bull, a goat, or a bird. Then they would lay their hands on the animal's head, symbolic of transferring their sins to the creature, which was put to death in their place. Their sins were then atoned for or covered, and a way was made for every sinner to be accepted by God.

Ten generations after Adam, Noah must have also been instructed in these laws as well because immediately after the catastrophic flood that destroyed nearly the entire human race he offered up sin sacrifices from the animals God had preserved.

"Then Noah built an altar to the LORD, and took of every clean animal and of every clean bird, and offered burnt offerings on the altar" (Gen 8:20).

Another ten generations after Noah, God called and chose Abraham to work His plan. From him God made a great nation (Israel) and blessed all other peoples of the earth through him. When Abraham was very old God asked him to sacrifice his only son Isaac. We know that God does not approve of human sacrifice, but He tested Abraham's obedience. When Isaac asked his father where the animal sacrifice (a lamb) was for the burnt offering, notice Abraham's response: *"My son, God will provide for Himself the lamb for a burnt offering" (Gen 22:8).* This was a prophetic statement concerning the future sacrifice of the Lamb of God, Jesus Christ, God's only Son, whom God would provide to be the final sacrifice for man's sin. God made a covenant with Abraham and because he had not withheld his only son from God, likewise centuries later God would not withhold His only Son from mankind. So we see that both Abraham and his young son Isaac understood the law of sacrifice as being necessary to nullify the effects of the law of sin and death.

Since the entire nation of Israel was guilty of breaking God's laws, God also commanded Moses, generations after Abraham, to make an altar and offer burnt offerings (Ex 20:24). In the Old Testament all worship centered around an altar of sacrifice.

So beginning with Adam and Eve, their children, and the generations that followed to Noah, Abraham, and Moses the law of sin and death along with the law of sacrifice was understood by all of Israel and perpetuated through each generation even after Moses.

Throughout the Old Testament the law of sin and death was continually in effect and continually nullified when the law of sacrifice was applied. The shed blood of innocent animals was to appease the wrath of God against sinners. This was God's plan. However, when this law of sacrifice was not applied plagues would break out and destroy the people. For example, in 2 Samuel 24 David had sinned against the Lord by taking a census of the nation. As a result, the wrath of God was unleashed throughout the nation in a plague that killed 70,000 people. Word came to David to offer up sacrificial animal blood offerings so the plague could be stopped.

"And David built there an altar to the LORD, and offered burnt offerings and peace offerings. So the LORD heeded the prayers for the land, and the plague was withdrawn from Israel" (2 Sam 24:25).

In Numbers 16 the same thing happened. After the rebellion of Korah when the ground opened up and swallowed people alive, the children of Israel complained against Moses and Aaron accusing them of killing the Lord's people. Notice what followed.

"And the LORD spoke to Moses, saying, "Get away from among this congregation, that I may consume them in a moment." And they fell on their faces. So Moses said to Aaron, "Take a censer and put fire in it from the altar, put incense on it, and take it quickly to the congregation and make atonement for them; for wrath has gone out from the LORD. The plague has begun." Then Aaron took it as Moses commanded, and ran into the midst of the assembly; and already the plague had begun among the people. So he put in the incense and made atonement for the people. And he stood between the dead and the living; so the plague was stopped. Now those who died in the plague were fourteen thousand seven hundred, besides those who died in the Korah incident. So Aaron returned to Moses at the door of the tabernacle of meeting, for the plague had stopped" (Num 16:44-50).

The incense Aaron offered was taken from the fire of the altar of burnt offerings where sacrifices for sin were continually made. The fire was symbolic of the blood atonement. Aaron's mediation had appeased the wrath of God. Actually, the appeasement of the wrath of God is tied up in a New Testament word called "propitiation".

"And He Himself is the propitiation for our sins, and not for ours only but also for the whole world" (1 John 2:2).

Propitiation, according to its Biblical use, means to appease or pacify the wrath of God against guilty sinners deserving of judgment, and turn that wrath into divine favor.

We know that Old Testament sacrifices were a foreshadowing of Jesus Christ, the Lamb of God who became the final sacrifice for the sins of the world. Born supernaturally of a virgin His blood was pure and sinless for it was in fact God's blood (Acts 20:28). The blood of an unblemished animal could only cover man's sin, but could not remove it. *"It is impossible for the blood of bulls and goats to take away sins" (Heb 10:4).* However, the blood of the sinless, spotless Lamb of God, who unlike animals, was created in the image of God, not only covers and forgives man's sin, but cleanses it, removes it, and delivers man from the power and dominion of it.

The key aspect of the crucifixion of Jesus Christ was that it satisfied the claims of divine justice for the punishment of man's sin. Jesus was the substitutionary sacrifice in that He took our place (Rom 8:3, 2 Cor 5:21, Gal 3:13). Rather than the crude pagan concept of appeasing the vengeful gods' unreasonable demands, propitiation will be forever tied to a perfect righteousness demanded by a holy and just God. Then that same righteousness was fully provided by God's love for lost mankind by sending His Son to be the propitiation for their sins.

"In this is love, not that we loved God, but that He loved us and sent His Son to be the propitiation for our sins" (1 John 4:10).

It was because of the love of God (John 3:16, Eph 5:2) that Jesus became our substitute for sin's penalty. The beauty and majesty of the cross is that we see both the judgment and the love of God being displayed there. God pronounced judgment on sin, but because of His love He paid for it Himself through His Son (Rom 5:8). This can be likened to a judge in a courtroom who brings down the gavel and sentences a criminal to the death penalty, but then he removes his judge's robe and takes the criminal's place in the punishment of his crime. God is both a Judge and a Savior. This is the wonder of the cross made plain. Jesus, the Son of God, who is perfectly righteous, holy, pure, and far above us in all His divine attributes, became man and bore the wrath of God on behalf of all hell-deserving sinners, enduring the horrific torture of the cross at the hands of those same sinners, all for their benefit! Sin was judged by a love that gave His life, gave His blood, and gave His all.

This is the meaning of the cross. God's love satisfied the demands of divine justice. Jesus Christ, the sinless, spotless Lamb of God, was crushed under the wrath of God (Isa 53:4-5) that you and I deserved so that we might be reconciled to God. Jesus died for the sins of the ungodly to save us from the wrath of God so that we could have peace with God. When anyone receives this revelation it will melt their heart and impact their life forever.

What a glorious plan to save the world! It makes no sense to the carnal mind. In fact, the Bible says it is foolishness to some:

"For the message of the cross is foolishness to those who are perishing, but to us who are being saved it is the power of God" (1 Cor 1:18).

"For since, in the wisdom of God, the world through wisdom did not know God, it pleased God through the foolishness of the message preached to save those who believe. For Jews request a sign, and Greeks seek after wisdom; but we preach Christ crucified, to the Jews a stumbling block and to the Greeks foolishness, but to those who are called, both Jews and Greeks, Christ the power of God and the wisdom of God" (1 Cor 1:21-24).

The Jews asked for a sign and miracles but instead got a crucified Messiah. This was a stumbling block and a scandal to them for they could not believe that a Savior and Messiah could be cursed on a cross. Their law stated, "Cursed is he who hangs on a tree (Deut 21:22-23)." Only the worst of criminals were subject to such treatment and torture. How could the Messiah be a criminal? The cross was an upside down plan, a mystery that could not be understood and received by the proud Jews. On the other hand, the Greeks (Gentiles) sought wisdom and philosophy as the means of discovering truth. To them the cross was foolishness or moronic (as one translation reads). It made no sense and did not appeal to their reasoning powers. Yet it is what God chose to save all of mankind and recover the universe.

I find no fault in Him.

Glory to His name forever!

Chapter 5

THE GOSPEL OF POWER

"Jesus power —super, super power! Satan power —powerless power!" –
Words to an African song

*"Maximum damage is done to the kingdom of darkness and maximum
blessing is done to advance the kingdom of light when miracles accompany
it's messengers."* – Author

**"So they went out and preached that people should repent. And
they cast out many demons, and anointed with oil many who were
sick, and healed them" (Mk 6:12-13).**

**"Then He began to rebuke the cities in which most of His mighty
works had been done, because they did not repent" (Mat 11:20).**

The demonstration of God's power in signs, wonders, and miracles
is a major part of the gospel and actually sets the tone for the demands
of Christ. You really have no right to demand repentance without
demonstrating the power of God. Taking up the cross seems like an
unreasonable demand except following a miracle. Jesus rebuked the
cities pronouncing woes on the people who did not repent after
witnessing His mighty works.

**"Woe to you, Chorazin! Woe to you, Bethsaida! For if the mighty
works which were done in you had been done in Tyre and Sidon, they
would have repented long ago in sackcloth and ashes.   But I say to**

65

you, it will be more tolerable for Tyre and Sidon in the day of judgment than for you. And you, Capernaum, who are exalted to heaven, will be brought down to Hades; for if the mighty works which were done in you had been done in Sodom, it would have remained until this day. But I say to you that it shall be more tolerable for the land of Sodom in the day of judgment than for you" (Mat 11:21-24).

In the above scripture Jesus infers that mighty works give people a greater opportunity to respond to the gospel, but also a greater condemnation on those who reject Him. To whom much is given much is required (Lk 12:48). According to Jesus, even Sodom and Gomorrah, that wicked city, would've repented and not been burned to the ground had they witnessed His mighty works (Mat 10:15). Therefore they will be judged less severely in the day of judgment than the cities where mighty works were done without ensuing repentance.

When Jesus sent out His disciples He gave them power over demons and disease (Mat 10:1). He equipped them with an ability and authority to demonstrate the power of God. Without it the gospel is incomplete.

"And as you go, preach, saying, 'The kingdom of heaven is at hand.' Heal the sick, cleanse the lepers, raise the dead, cast out demons. Freely you have received, freely give" (Mat 10:7-8).

Notice in this context that Jesus did not tell His disciples to *pray* for the sick, the lepers, the dead, and the demon possessed. He commanded them to *heal* the sick, cleanse the lepers, resurrect the dead, and deliver the demon possessed. In other words, Jesus authorized them to heal the sick, not pray for the sick. Of course, it is scriptural to pray for the sick (Jam 5:14), but it's interesting that in the gospels and in the book of Acts we don't find one reference to praying for the sick. This tells me that these early apostles had an understanding of the authority they'd been given in a way that much of the Church and its ministers today do not.

It was Jesus' purpose that the supernatural power of God would signal the kingdom of heaven's arrival. His purpose has not changed. We who are followers of Jesus can expect to do the same. The power is in the proclamation. He commands us to say, "The kingdom of heaven is here!" He authorizes you to confirm it with power. God will back you up. Act and you will see.

A few years ago I traveled to an interior city in Sierra Leone, West Africa to minister. Upon arrival my hosts escorted me to go see some city officials. When I stepped into the female mayor's office I was met by approximately 20 of her staff. I asked the Lord what kind of introduction I should give. He told me to proclaim that the kingdom of heaven had come to their city and to heal the sick in the mayor's office. I asked for a show of hands of who was sick, and instructed them to put their hands on their own bodies, and then commanded them to be healed. Several testified of being instantly healed either through pain leaving their bodies or being alleviated from an afflicted condition. The mayor then told me that I could do anything I wanted to do in the city, that it was my city, and they would give me any assistance I needed.

Kingdom authority can stir up persecution or command instant favor, or both. In this case, we received great favor. They recognized that God was with me. The bolder you are the more results you will see.

Until the power of God is demonstrated the gospel has not been fully preached.

"For I will not dare to speak of any of those things which Christ has not accomplished through me, in word and deed, to make the

Gentiles obedient—in mighty signs and wonders, by the power of the Spirit of God, so that from Jerusalem and round about to Illyricum I have <u>fully preached the gospel of Christ</u>" (Rom 15:18-19).

Paul said the Gentiles were persuaded to obedience by his full presentation of the gospel in mighty signs and wonders. His preaching was accompanied by the power of the Spirit of God, and it triggered a faith response from the Gentiles.

Paul made another similar statement: *"And my speech and my preaching were not with persuasive words of human wisdom, but in demonstration of the Spirit and of power, that your faith should not be in the wisdom of men but in the power of God" (1 Cor 2:4-5).*

Paul put no confidence in his own persuasive words to convince men of the gospel. He did not preach philosophy, psychology, or a soulical brand of speech consisting of man's wisdom that is so common today. He did not want men's faith to be based on his eloquence or fleshly wisdom. He avoided a man-centered gospel, but placed all his confidence in the demonstration of God's Spirit and power to draw men to Christ.

From Genesis to Revelation the scriptures are full of miracles and a display of the power of God. The Bible is a supernatural book. The public ministry of Jesus Christ, His disciples, and that of the early Church were marked by demonstrations and manifestations of the power of God. People are not saved by the miraculous. They are saved by hearing words of the gospel (Acts 11:14, Rom 10:14), but the miraculous is an attention-getter and a "dinner bell" to let people know that something great is happening. It convinces people of the reality of God. Let's examine some accounts in the book of Acts to see the effects of the power of God.

First of all, the initial outpouring of the Holy Spirit was supernatural when men spoke in languages never learned and the Jews from other nations understood them (Acts 2). This was a unique miracle. Results: After hearing Peter preach, 3,000 new souls were added to the church and others were added daily thereafter (Acts 2:41, 47).

Next, Peter and John, by the authority of the name of Jesus, heal a man lame from birth (Acts 3). Results: 5,000 men believed after hearing the gospel (Acts 4:4). Of course, persecution broke out immediately. The church prayed and the place of assembly shook, and they were all filled with the Holy Spirit and spoke the Word of God boldly (Acts 4:31).

Then, we come to a most compelling account regarding Ananias and Sapphira, a married couple in the church who came under the judgment of God and died for lying to the Holy Spirit. This is what has been referred to as a judgment miracle. Results: Great fear came on the church and all who heard of it (Acts 5:5, 11). The apostles then performed many more signs and wonders (Acts 5:12). Results: Multitudes of men and women were increasingly added to the Lord, and came to Jerusalem from the surrounding cities bringing the sick and tormented (Acts 5:14-16). Of course, persecution followed. The devil hates the manifestation of the power of God and will vigorously oppose it because by it people are drawn to the gospel.

Stephen who was full of faith and power began to do great wonders and signs among the people (Acts 6:8). Results: Persecution – what else? Stephen was martyred (Acts 7) and the subsequent result was that Saul, whom Stephen prayed forgiveness for, and who later became Paul, was gloriously converted and became the greatest apostle of the early Church (Acts 9). As a result of the persecution, the church was scattered and went everywhere preaching the Word (Acts 8:3-4).

Philip also moved in the miraculous. The results: The people heard him attentively, and an entire city was impacted by the gospel and filled with great joy (Acts 8:5-8). By the way, both Philip and Stephen were not original apostles, for those who believe miracles passed away with the apostles.

Saul had a life-changing encounter with the Lord (Acts 9). Ananias, also not an original apostle, was sent by supernatural revelation to minister to Saul (the Lord told Ananias specifically where Saul was, what he was going through, and the purpose of God for his life). Results: All who heard of Saul's conversion were amazed because they knew him before as the greatest persecutor of the Church. Not long after Saul started preaching the Jews plotted to kill him. Of course, what else? If the devil can't stop you he will try and kill you.

Still in Acts 9 Peter heals a paralyzed man. Results: All who saw the man in two different cities turned to the Lord (v 32-35). Then Peter goes to another city and raises a woman from the dead. Results: This became known throughout the area and many believed on the Lord (v 42).

Acts 10 and 11 is a long account of how God opened the door of the gospel to the Gentiles. Once again, miraculous things took place through revelation and power. Results: The Gentiles received the gospel and the Holy Spirit fell on them (Acts 10:44-46).

In Acts 12 after Herod killed James with the sword He had Peter arrested and put in prison. An angel then delivered him supernaturally.

Beginning in Acts 13 Paul and Barnabas were separated for missionary work. From that point on we see Paul dominating the spiritual landscape in the second portion of the book of Acts as the Holy Spirit highlighted his ministry exploits. The supernatural power of God accompanied him even as he testified in the scriptures above.

The pattern is the same throughout the entire book of Acts which is the genesis of the Church and God's blueprint for it. The power of the gospel usually resulted in either revivals or riots or both. It produced conversions and crisis. It caused joy and jeer. It made many people glad and others mad. It brought astonishment and animosity. Maximum damage is done to the kingdom of darkness, and maximum blessing is done to advance the kingdom of light, when miracles accompany its messengers.

"And these signs shall follow those who believe...And they went out and preached everywhere, the Lord working with them and confirming the Word through accompanying signs" (Mk 16:17, 20).

Years ago I was preaching in a small church in Dakar, Senegal, a 90% Islamic nation. At the end of one particular meeting a Senegalese man came forward and asked the local pastor if he and I could come to his house to minister to his sick wife. She was very weak and in pain, and her mobility was extremely limited. She could not lay down flat in her bed or walk very far. The man told us that he had gone to witchdoctors and paid money to have her healed, but she had only gotten worse.

When we arrived at this man's house we found his wife just as he had explained to us. I asked her if she believed Jesus Christ could heal her. After replying in the affirmative I anointed her with oil and asked her to do something she couldn't do before. As she began walking and bending, all her pain and symptoms disappeared. But the story gets even better.

After I had left the country I received an email on the background and progress that this man and his family had made in the faith. I discovered that this man was formerly a gangster for the devil. He would gather young men and send them to churches to harass and trouble them in various ways. Even the Muslims in his neighborhood and area were afraid of him. However, when his wife was healed and experienced the power of God this man began to testify of Jesus. In the email I received, it reported that he was telling the Muslims such things as: *"You are all blind and fooling yourselves! Jesus Christ is the Son of God!"* I've lived in Islamic nations as a missionary, and I can tell you that no one makes bold statements like that for fear of offending the Muslims for they adamantly deny Jesus as the Son of God. In some nations such statements can even get you killed.

When God's power touches someone it often sets them on fire and makes them fearless. The woman at the well left her waterpot (because she had just received the living water) and went into the city and testified to the men of Jesus (John 4:28-30). Considering her immoral reputation and the cultural restrictions of male and female interaction during that day this was a bold act by this woman. But she had been touched with God's fire and could not keep her mouth shut.

Similarly, the leper whom Jesus cleansed and made whole, and then told him not to tell anyone of his miracle (Mk 1:40-45) went wild and *"blazed abroad the matter"*. He, too was set on fire through a miracle and could not keep quiet.

When the apostles were threatened repeatedly by city and religious authorities they replied, **"We cannot but speak the things which we have seen and heard" (Acts 4:20).** In the Greek this literally means: "We don't have any ability to keep silent." An encounter with God's power can make zealots and fanatics out of all of us. A raw holy enthusiasm seems to take over one who has been mightily touched by God. "In order to stop me you got to kill me" seems to be the unshakeable attitude of one who has had an encounter with God's presence and power that swallows up all inhibitions and fears.

When the fire of God burned in the prophet Jeremiah he exclaimed: *"Then I said, I will not make mention of Him, nor speak anymore in His name. But His word was in my heart like a burning fire shut up in my bones; I was weary of holding it back, and I could not"* (Jer 20:9).

Jeremiah tried to keep quiet but couldn't. He tried *not* to mention God's name, but he couldn't. He tried *not* to preach His Word, but he couldn't. The burning fire of God in him was too great.

This Senegalese man's transformation was evident to all who knew him before in his former life. Just as the apostle Paul, the faith he once persecuted he now preached. It was also reported to me that he started a Bible study in his house and his entire family was converted. This is the purpose of signs, wonders, and miracles. One miracle can set a person on fire and change him forever, but it can also affect an entire neighborhood, community, a city, and even a nation.

"For our gospel did not come to you in word only, but also in power, and in the Holy Spirit and in much assurance, as you know what kind of men we were among you for your sake" (1 Thes 1:5).

Today there are many skeptics, doubters, and mockers concerning miracles and the power of God. There are those who say miracles passed away in the first century with the last apostle. Then there are those that slander and demean miracle workers who operate in the supernatural power of God. Satan uses some people as his puppets to spew forth such criticism because he fears miracles, signs, and wonders because they testify of Jesus Christ, reveal the Father God (John 10:25), and set souls on fire with the final result being that others are drawn to Jesus and to His great salvation.

Satan has hoodwinked many churches today and cheated them out of the power of God through their own unbelief. These powerless churches have ceased to be a threat to Satan. If an army of soldiers go to battle without weaponry and artillery they are not a threat to the enemy. Likewise, it is with these churches. After the resurrection Jesus commanded His disciples to wait for the promise of the Holy Spirit so that they could receive power (Acts 1:8). In other words, they were not to go and attempt to do God's work without it.

"As the Father has sent Me, I also send you" (John 20:21). In the same way the heavenly Father sent Jesus in power, so now Jesus sends us. Without the power of the gospel we cannot be effective witnesses. Preach the gospel and preach it with power! Why settle for anything less?

Chapter 6

THE MESSAGE OF THE CROSS
TESTIMONY

This is a testimony from a good friend of mine who carries a wooden cross and does open air evangelistic ministry. I emboldened the words that were emboldened in his original testimony. This is an example of using the different aspects of the gospel as well the Law to bring men to Christ.

Recently a friend of mine came to our home for a one night visit and some open air ministry at Lowes Motor Speedway. We loaded up the big cross and went to the Speedway where they were having an enormous car show and sale. We saw thousands of people walking around, looking at cars, etc.

We noticed that the largest crowds of people were those who were gathered at the crosswalk just across from the main entrance to the Speedway. So we decided to set up the big 10 foot cross right there in order to arrest their attention to the message of the cross. What better place to set up a huge cross and preach the gospel!

The State Highway Patrol was there directing the very heavy traffic, and they would hold the people for up to 10 minutes at a time to allow vehicle traffic to flow smoothly during this big event.

As we raised up the big cross and began to preach, my friend and I were both astonished at the fact that it seemed that everyone was listening intently to the message. People weren't talking among themselves, no one heckled, and nobody cursed at us. They all just quietly listened to the message as we drew attention to the big cross, and our reason for being out there preaching.

I told them that God Almighty had separated all those who hear the message of the cross into 2 categories:

1) Those who see the cross as foolishness. These are the people who perish which means they will spend a long forever in the **lake of fire**, which is the second death. I warned, urged, and encouraged them not to be in that group.

2) Those who are saved. To these, and these only, the message of the cross is the power of God! This is the only attitude and response to the message that can be acceptable to God.

We told them that the cross of Christ was necessary for two primary reasons:

1) We are all part of the ultimate statistic: 10 out of every 10 people die! In fact, in the next 24 hours 146,000 people will die around the world. No one gets out of this world alive.

2) We have all broken God's Law, which the Bible says is holy, just, good, and perfect.

I told them that God **has an obligation** to uphold His Law and make it honorable. That *"...He can in no wise clear the guilty"*. He cannot set aside the execution of the penalty for breaking His Law in showing mercy to those who are guilty of breaking it.

I reasoned with the people concerning their **guilt for having sinned** against such a righteous, good, and holy Creator. I reasoned with them that everyone knows it is wrong to lie especially when someone lies to them or about them.

I tried to make them see that everyone knows it is wrong to steal especially when someone steals from them! And everyone understands how wrong it is to commit adultery when their spouse does it! But Jesus Christ pointed out that whenever someone looks with lust, they commit adultery with that person already in their heart!

I expounded briefly of **God's righteous judgment** in threatening **eternal wrath and endless punishment** against His enemies. Then I explained that the **only way** in which God could **wisely** and **justly** offer pardon and forgiveness to guilty sinners was to offer up His own Son as an **innocent substitute**, in order to satisfy the awful demands of the justice and vengeance due those who violated God's just commands. I told them that **the sufferings of Christ** make it possible and **wise** and **just** and **good** for God to pardon and forgive the sinner, whenever he **turns away from his own way and believes the good news**, yielding himself in full and **complete love** and **obedience** to the **mercy** and **grace of God** with **faith in the blood of Jesus Christ** as the **only** remedy for sin and damnation.

I pointed out that God requires that we all believe the **Gospel** "good news" that **Jesus died** for **our sins, was buried and raised again the third day.** And that when God the Father raised up His Son Jesus from the dead He broke the **power of sin and death** over all those who **repent and believe the gospel.**

I knew I had only 5-10 minutes to speak to each group, so I said these things in the most plain, pointed, and personal manner possible.

As we continued to preach, we watched as the faces of these precious people would show deep conviction, as if they were thinking, *"Hey this actually makes sense! I have offended God! I deserve to be sent to the lowest hell! But God is willing to show me mercy if I will only repent, believe, and obey the gospel of His Son!"*

We stayed there approximately 5 hours, and we estimated that we preached over 40 times to an average new crowd of between 25-50 people each. It was perhaps the most fun I have had open air preaching in many years!

TO GOD BE ALL THE GLORY, HONOR, AND PRAISE!

Chapter 7

A CHRISTMAS LETTER

A PRESENTATION OF THE GOSPEL

This is a copy of a Christmas letter I wrote and mailed out years ago to 60 individuals and families who lived in our apartment complex. This is another example of including the various components of the gospel in our preaching and testimony. Feel free to use all or any portion of it to reach souls.

Dear Friends,

Merry Christmas!!! Let us remember to keep the "Christ" in Christmas. There are many who would like to "X" the Christ and celebrate X-mas.

Listen to this statement: Christ is the greatest central fact in the world's history. To him everything looks forward or backward. All the lines of history converge upon Him. All the great purposes of God culminate in Him. The greatest and most momentous fact that the history of the world records is Christ's birth.

Christmas is celebrated because of this one verse of Scripture: *"She will give birth to a Son and you are to give Him the name Jesus [short for "the Lord is salvation"], because He will save His people from their sins"* *(Mat 1:21).*

Friend, sin is the great problem of the human race and the Scriptures teach us that hell is the penalty for sin. But salvation is more than an exit visa to heaven; it is freedom from sin now in this life.

Christmas has very little meaning or significance without this transformation in our hearts.

Please allow me to tell you my story: My old life was one of pain and pleasure. Some pain and then some pleasure; more pain and then more pleasure. I found out that my sinful life really had no happiness; just fighting off unhappiness. I was a social drinker, a womanizer (being gay is the equivalent; God calls it sin – Leviticus 18:22), a blasphemer (using God's name in vain), full of lust (if you even fantasize of a sexual relationship outside of marriage the Bible calls you an adulterer), full of greed, full of anger, and full of bitterness. I fell short of God's commandments, and so has every human being. *"There is none righteous, no, not one..." (Rom 3:10).*

Yet I was a semi-regular church goer, prayed to God, and counted myself a part of the good citizens of this country. Like so many today I was trusting in my good works to save me. **If you are hoping for good works to save you, you are trusting in a parachute that is full of holes.** On judgment day you will crash and burn. We have all sinned against God our Creator. If any of us are not convinced of that, then it will take hell to convince us.

Death is as sure as taxes, if not surer. In this life is the only chance we will get to let go of our sins and turn to Christ. That is true repentance. To an old soldier it means, "Attention! Halt! About turn... quick march!" **If you haven't let go of your sins, you are holding onto a grenade with the pin pulled out.**

If Satan sees your interest in Christ, I warn you that he will try and kill you to keep you from this great salvation. If he sees that you're not interested he'll kill you anyway, and you'll spend eternity in hell. Forever.

The Good News is that Christ died on the cross and shed His Holy Blood to pay the penalty for our sins and then He rose again triumphant (Besides Christmas, Easter is the second most celebrated holiday – think about that). On the cross of Jesus Christ was the greatest demonstration of love and mercy that mankind has ever been shown. It was there that the Lord Jesus suffered, bled, and died so that man could receive the power of a transformed heart and a new life.

What must you do? Turn to Christ now, friend and be saved from your sins. Then and only then can you know the true meaning of Christmas.

Merry Christmas or Miserable Christmas?

Which will it be?

Instructions: *Right now, in your heart, cry out to God to save you from your sins by the Blood of Jesus. Right now, with your mouth, ask Him to deliver you from the snare of the devil and to make you His own. Give up your sinful self-will and turn back to God. Die to your own will and your own life. Jesus Christ will deliver you and give you a new life. Put your faith in Him.*

For prayer or counsel please call _____. Let us know if you've turned to Christ by calling us or writing to us. Remember, God loves you and we love you.

P.S. Notice this letter makes no appeal for money or the sale of any product. It is written out of a deep sincerity and a pure love for your soul. Please know that we are praying for you to know Christ.

ABOUT THE AUTHOR

Bert M. Farias, together with his wife, Carolyn, graduates of Rhema Bible Training Center, founded Holy Fire Ministries in 1997 after serving for nine years as missionaries in West Africa, establishing nation-changing interdenominational Bible training centers with an organization called Living Word Missions.

From 1999 to 2003, Bert served as the internship coordinator on the senior leadership team of the Brownsville Revival School of Ministry and Fire School of Ministry in Pensacola, Florida, a school birthed from a massive, heaven-sent revival that brought approximately four million visitors from around the world, with an estimated 150,000 first-time conversions. There, Rev. Farias and his wife taught and mentored young men and women in the call of God and trained them for the work of the ministry.

Bert is a messenger of the Lord carrying a spirit of revival to the Church and the nations. An anointing of fire marks his ministry with frequent demonstrations of the Spirit and the power of God. With a divine commission to also write, Bert has authored several books with an emphasis on helping to restore the true spirit of Christianity in the Church today and preparing the saints for the glory of God, the harvest, and the imminent return of the Lord.

Before being dedicated solely to the full-time preaching and teaching ministry, Bert experienced a unique and powerful baptism of fire. His consuming passion is for human beings to come into a real and vibrant relationship with the Lord Jesus Christ through the power of the Holy Spirit and to become passionate workers in His kingdom, thus preparing them for the second coming of Christ, being among the wise virgins and a part of the first-fruits harvest who will gain an abundant entrance into glory and receive a sure reward.

Bert currently resides in Windham, New Hampshire, with his beautiful wife, Carolyn. They are proud parents of one precious son of promise.

OTHER BOOKS BY BERT M. FARIAS

SOULISH LEADERSHIP

This book is for everyone...

- Who longs for purity of heart.
- Who desires to be set aright in the core of his being.
- Who dreads God's disapproval more than man's.
- Whose greatest phobia is the fear of a wasted life and burned-up works.

The works that endure the testing of God's holy fire will one day be rewarded. Others will suffer loss (1 Cor 3:12-15). Will your works stand the fire or will they go up in smoke? In that day the motive of every heart will be made clear. Leaders will be judged by a higher standard. Only one question will matter then, and it's the same question that matters now: Are you building your kingdom or the kingdom of God?

THE JOURNAL OF A JOURNEY TO HIS HOLINESS

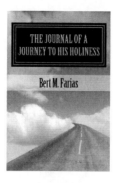

This journal-style book is not your normal run-of-the-mill literary work. Rather, it is a mystery from heaven unveiled---a saving word----a blueprint of the mind of God for every minister and saint. This journal will take you to a school beyond the veil wherein the Holy Spirit himself is the instructor.

The content of this journal reads like a tapestry woven by an unseen hand into the multi-colored fabric of each page. Its timeless truths and priceless principles will demand your prayerful attention; indeed a rare find for this day and age.

Don't just read this journal, but let it read you. Allow it to impregnate you with a depth of holy desire for intimacy and unbroken fellowship with the Father of spirits. There is a great purging and cleansing God wants to do in this hour in his Church, especially among ministers. This journal is one of those sign-posts that definitely point the way.

THE REAL SPIRIT OF REVIVAL

In this book, Bert challenges the status quo of Christianity today and redefines its true spirit which is one of revival and of living the Spirit filled life. With one eye on the coming glory of the Lord and His soon return, and another eye on the harvest of souls yet to be reached, *The Real Spirit Of Revival* takes the reader into a preparation to becoming a true lover of Jesus and a passionate worker in His kingdom. These vital truths that dot each new chapter of this book are sure to awaken you as one from a deep sleep, and light a fire in your soul.

If you are tired of a mundane relationship with God and desire to burn with His holy fire this book is a must read.

PURITY OF HEART

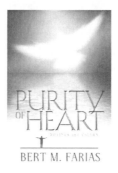

The primary basis of all judgment concerning the deeds done in our bodies is our motives. Our values determine our motives, and our motives are the real reason behind our thoughts, words, and deeds. Only God can see the true motives of every man's heart.

Almost all human beings have something to hide. Nearly everyone twists words, events, and situations to their own advantage, to place themselves in the best possible light. Men often have ulterior motives and hidden agendas. This is sin and a form of hiding.

Adam and Eve first hid from the presence of the Lord in the garden after they had fallen. But there will be no hiding from the presence of the Lord on that solemn Day of Judgment.

Purity of Heart will prepare you for that day and spare you loss at the judgment seat of Christ so that you may receive your full reward. What is done in pure love, by the leading of the Spirit, and for the glory and honor of God shall reap the fullest rewards.

THE REAL SALVATION

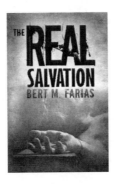

Can you imagine feeling secure in a salvation you don't even possess? Such is the state of mass humanity today. We have libraries full of sermons yet still so much confusion and deception about what the real salvation is. With poignancy and pinpoint clarity this short and sweet book cuts through the fat of satanic philosophy, exposes the deception of the broad way of religion, and shines the light on the narrow path to eternal life. Most books are 200 pages with 30 pages worthwhile, and 170 of fluff. *The Real Salvation* is less than 60 pages, but every word counts. Make it count for you and your unsaved friends and loved ones!

MY SON, MY SON

This book is one of the most unique books on father-son relationships you will ever find. Co-written by father and son, it has a personal touch and intimate tone that will leave you teary-eyed one moment and then rejoicing the next. Within its pages you will find a spiritual quality of training and a godly example of shepherding children that will both enrich and empower parents. It also offers hope for those parents who have fallen short or started late in their child training.

Experience the power and the promise of fathers who fear the Lord.

Fathers, your son (or daughter) is typically in your home for an average of 18-20 years before he ventures out independently to navigate his own little boat in this world's turbulent waters. Until then, with God's help, you, more than anyone else, have the greatest opportunity to shape him and mold him into the man he will eventually become. You've got one shot at being a father.

Make it count.

Prayer: The Language Of The Spirit is a short and poignant book that helps lay a foundation from the Word for knowing and walking with God. Each chapter directs the earnest believer into possessing a life of communion with God and praying without ceasing.

Prayer is walking with God. It is habitual fellowship with God. You can walk so close to God that you feel like you're in heaven. The key that will move you toward this richness of communion with Him is to not only know the Word but to cultivate a receptivity and sensitivity to His Spirit and presence.

You can experience this kind of life in God if you will pursue Him. It all begins with receiving the baptism of the Holy Spirit and praying extensively in other tongues. This is the language of the Spirit.

PASSING ON THE MOVE OF GOD

TO THE NEXT GENERATION

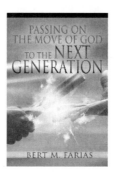

This book, *Passing on the Move of God to the Next Generation*, is like a template for the New Testament Church. Its words act as a plumb line that will help restore the uncompromised Word and the fullness of the Spirit back to our pulpits and churches.

When we compare the Word that the early apostles preached and that of our more recent Pentecostal forefathers, we find a depth and richness rarely evidenced today. Additionally, there was also an understanding and accuracy in spiritual operations that are clearly missing from normal Pentecostal and Charismatic experience in this generation.

But there is a hunger stirring at our spiritual tables, and a thirst screaming out from the deep wells that have been dug from past fathers of the faith. Can you hear the winds of God blowing and the sound of the abundance of rain?

Bert Farias blows the trumpet loud and clear, summoning the Church and its preachers to return to the authenticity of the Scriptures and their Pentecostal roots of Spirit and fire (Acts 2). If we heed this call, it can turn the tide of ignorance, apathy, and compromise and flood our churches again with the real move of the Holy Spirit.